SHAPE NOTE SINGING

Lauren Turner

Shape Note Singing ©2021 by **Lauren Turner**. Published in the United States by Vegetarian Alcoholic Press. Not one part of this work may be reproduced without expressed written consent from the author. For more information, please contact vegalpress@gmail.com

Cover art by Sally Anne Morgan, Rat Bee Press

for Trevor

CONTENTS

Hymnology	9
Skittish of Our Own Wilderness: A Preface	11
EAR PIECES (after Pauline Oliveros)	
I.	21
II.	23
III.	25

SHAPE NOTES

Cul-de-sac	29
Ecclesiastes	30
I Was the Exalted Exhale	32
Disembodied Sonnet	33
Disembodied Sestina	34
Will the Circle Be Unbroken?	36
Hatching	37
Slow Morning Crow	38
Alarmist Apology	39
Ad Tendere: An Elegy for David Berman	40
Transaction In Technicolor	42
Let There Be	44

SOURCES

ACKNOWLEDGEMENTS

"Listen to everything all the time and remind yourself when you are not listening."
—**Pauline Oliveros**

"We cannot live in a world that is interpreted for us by others. An interpreted world is not a hope. Part of the terror is to take back our own listening. To use our own voice. To see our own light."
—**Hildegard of Bingen**

Hymnology

While they're off measuring the upward mobility of the folksong, I study hymnology. We spend a week on Sacred Harp singing. A sacred harp is a human voice, sounding off in shapes that anyone can reach. Four shapes: a right triangle for *fa*, an oval for *sol*, a rectangle for *la*, and a diamond for *mi*. These shape notes morph; stretch to widen the gulf between the most disparate versions of "Amazing Grace" you've ever heard, while the professor's face clouds over. "Did you all know that John Newton—the composer of 'Amazing Grace'—was a slave trader?" The cloud now palpable as students take notes with sharp pencils on crisp notebook paper. "It could only be penned from that low of a place, don't you think?" The pencils freeze. Disgust manifests in the only tool I have—that #2 graphite sketching shape notes of all geometrical dispositions in the margins of my notebook. I cease to listen to Newton's redemption story. I wonder what it would feel like if we sang in actual shapes when we discuss things like cultural appropriation or politics. *Ahhh*, we could sing, drawing a square on the map of our city. *Oooh*, you would go, watercoloring over the lines—suggesting spillage. And instead of arguing over who created rock & roll, we could *OH!* ourselves into a collective dizziness, like an audience in the wake of Elvis performing Sister Rosetta Tharpe's "Up Above My Head I Hear Music in the Air."

Skittish of Our Own Wilderness

"Attention is the beginning of devotion."
—Mary Oliver

The first week I had the cat, I immediately began questioning our tendencies. His and mine.

The cat was born into sickness—one of the only kittens of his litter to survive. He lost one eye to feline herpes virus, and the shelter I adopted from nursed the other back to health. Due to his history, I was especially vigilant. I didn't want to cause any further discomfort, but that became its own particular bind.

Observing him closely, I became more acutely aware of my own tendencies. When he clawed something he shouldn't, I watched myself from above as I did a series of things, including but not limited to: booping him on the nose, pulling or tossing him off of the surface in erratic desperation, and sternly raising my voice into a hard-lined *NO*. I googled *how to discipline a kitten* and learned within a few minutes of harried skimming that all of these things are big, fat, bad ideas. I began to despair that I'd be a bad cat mom. I began to despair that I'd be a bad… mom (maybe, someday).

The third day we had the cat, I became bottomlessly upset. Not at the cat. It was something my partner did—a small, unintentionally hurtful thing, and yet it reverberated into an abyss with a sharp, insistent echo. He came home from a bar with a friend much later than he said he would, which reminded me of another time earlier in the relationship when he'd come home late—a night when we agonized over our miscommunications for hours before deciding we needed to take a break. This time was much different, which he explained with patience—but it was too late. I'd associated coming home late with abandonment, and I was unreachable. I'd conflated the origin with the echo, and then, watching myself from above, I saw myself panic. This was not the first time.

> *I could not locate the origin of the echo.*
> *I could not locate the origin of the echo.*
> *I could not locate the origin of the echo.*

As soon as I calmed down, I found the cat. I lay down on the floor beside him and spoke through tears. I told him I hadn't meant to scare him with my outburst. He licked the tears clean off my nose.

The next day, back on the floor: I was playing with the cat. Oh, yes, I was there! Toes to pupils, engaged and locked in on the cat, ever engaged. My partner took a knee behind me and drew me close, said that while he was hurt from my overreaction—he loved me. *"My big love for you never goes away."* His lips brushed my ear. My whole body sighed itself further into his embrace. We then shifted our attention to the cat, which is to say that we became further devoted.

I received a book of Mary Oliver's essays, *Upstream,* from my partner's mother the week we brought home our kitten. I cracked it open while the kitten purred in my lap. Somewhere along the way, he began to lick my hand. We went on that way for a while, me reading and him licking. I wondered if he thought I was his mother and wanted to nurse. A wise friend told me it meant he felt I was part of his family. He was treating me the way his mother once treated him. I smiled at the irony—I'd expected that he needed my nurturing, but instead he was offering his. This reminded me of Mary Oliver's "Wild Geese" and its notion of belonging. Perhaps the cat was announcing my *"place / in the family of things"* with his tiny sandpaper tongue, singing:

> *You are an origin.*
> *You are an origin.*
> *You are an origin.*

I've been diagnosed with something called Religious Trauma Syndrome, which is a burgeoning corner of research that has not yet made it into the DSM-5. 'Diagnosed' is generous—my therapist at the time didn't feel we needed to parse it out much. I trusted she knew what was best, that perhaps fixating on a particular syndrome might be more limiting for my healing than helpful. But since then, I've discovered that researching this trauma syndrome can feel simultaneously productive and confusing.

While I may hold conflicting feelings about my loose diagnosis, I am comforted by having one because that means what I'm experiencing is nameable. That there are others that have charted this kind of pain, and they were also taught a particular belief about the world as if it were objective truth. And now we have trouble with what is true and what is dangerous. We become hyper-vigilant. Our wires cross. Our alarm systems sound off at strange times.

I could catalog the alarm sounds here—tell you about each one's particular tone and timbre—from the insistent and clanging rage to the dull, faint chime of unacknowledged guilt. I could tell you about being six years old and unable to fall asleep because I wanted to be absolutely certain that I wasn't going to burn in hell when I died, the pastor's words sounding the alarm through my addled brain: "Do you *know* that you *know* that you *know* that if you died tonight, you'd go to meet Jesus?"

I could tell you about learning the rules before even making it to the game; about being given all the answers before even having a question—before having a language for the asking.

I'm not as interested in mining my traumatic memories as I am in recognizing their role in a slow, insidious crawl toward growing up to feel like I wasn't the protagonist of my own life. I felt I needed permission to occupy my body, move around in it and make the earth my home and not simply camp out in it until Heaven or Hell claimed me. The sounds of this crawl—this bizarre and courageous journey—are kept in my library, my ever-changing control room, my world of triggers and receptors.

Surely, you have your own. There are so many things I could tell you—but this is a story about attention, about devotion.

In college, I came across philosopher-theologian Paul Tillich's definition of religion as "ultimate concern." When I first heard this, it felt like a new pathway of empathy was bubbling up beneath me, a possible movement to continue relating to my family and community, even amid the alarms. Tillich's definition in his book *Dynamics of Faith* opened up the possibility of one's religious identity meaning more than their doctrine, more like an embodied state: *"the state of being grasped by an ultimate concern, a concern which qualifies all other concerns as preliminary and which itself contains the answer to the question of the meaning of life."* What if our differences were more preliminary than they seemed? And if so, how could I move through them, precariously avoiding tripping my wires?

Religious trauma can look like questioning reality and its insistence on collapsing under the weight of your expectations. It can make it easy to forget unconditional love (or what my partner called *the big love)*, to accept your lack of rigid definitions for big things like love. It can make it difficult to trust yourself and others, and to listen. Truly listen. In a sense, I think my not-quite-diagnosis helps me to listen more closely.

The late composer Pauline Oliveros is best known for her theory of Deep Listening. In the introduction to her book "Deep Listening: The Composer's Guide to Sound Practice," she writes: *"Deep Listening is a practice that is intended to heighten and expand consciousness of sound in as many dimensions of awareness and attentional dynamics as humanly possible."* Oliveros proposes that there are two types of listening: *focal* (a conversation with a friend) and *global* (the birds flying overhead as you speak, the gravel underfoot as you walk together). Deep Listening seeks to do both, at once. This is something the cat knows.

Since becoming acquainted with Oliveros' work and beginning to play free improvised music in the experimental music communities of Nashville, listening has become an active way to engage with my particular trauma. Improvising is a vulnerable space, wild with possibility, hinging on trust and listening—both focally (to our own part, or to the lead) and globally (what the others are communicating via rhythm, melody, or energy; how our environment is responding to our sound with echo or overtone). When we listen well, we amuse ourselves with what harmonies arise and cohere. It isn't so austere—it's playful. I've discovered new ways of playing my instrument simply by learning to play along with my friends, playing theirs. The foregrounding of trust that takes place while improvising feels a lot like having a conversation with those whom I love.

Investigating Tillich's *faith as ultimate concern* liberates me to consider that my family's and my ultimate concerns—while practiced and performed distinctly—are in essence, deeply shared and foundational. We are each grasped by a concern for sharing kindness, peace, and *the big love*. When I'm listening deeply to the focal-global utterances of my family, this is what I hear—clear and beautiful, over any alarm. The practice of Deep Listening has gifted me with the posture for leaning into the ultimate concerns of myself and those I love, for acknowledging the discord and harmonies that arise as human and alive, instead of 'good' or 'bad.'

Mary Oliver writes in *Upstream*: *"In the beginning I was so young and such a stranger to myself I hardly existed. I had to go out in the world and see it and hear it and react to it, before I knew at all who I was, what I was, what I wanted to be."* A cultivation of curiosity, of listening, is what catalyzed her identity, in work and in life. I wonder if the stranger-self is only befriended once the rest of the world is befriended. It's got to be a lifelong befriending—sometimes beginning outward and reaching in, sometimes moving opposite. This is something else the cat knows.

Deep Listening is a practice of exploring while tethered to receptivity. Oliveros asserts that animals exemplify this best: *"When you enter an environment where there are [animals,] they are listening to you completely. You are received. Your presence may be the difference between life and death for the creatures of the environment. Listening is survival!"* When I sit outside for a listening meditation, I feel grateful to be received by these creatures as well as to receive their music. Our listening attention is both an act of compassion for another as well as for the self and its survival.

When I was a kid, my brother and I played a game called Tails. There were no rules, and no winners. All we had to do was find a blanket and tuck it into the back of our pants. We wanted to secure it well enough while leaving enough trailing down our backsides so it looked as if we had tails, of course. Next, we'd run around the room and sing, top volume: *"Tails, tails, tails, tails, tails!"* in a circular melody, like a round. We'd play for hours that way—full-tilt giggling, overjoyed by the simplicity of movement, of riffing off of one another, of tapping into our inner wilderness.

When Mary Oliver passed one year ago, all sorts of people came out with arms-a-swinging on the Internet. They emphasized Oliver's skill as a poet, that her poems were dark and complex, and she wasn't the Hallmark poet some folks thought her to be. I agreed with these tweets and articles, read them ravenously. However, I felt uneasy that these arms-a-swinging couldn't simply relax, holding the things they liked about Oliver with a secure warmth. That they felt they had to be on the offensive, or was it the defensive? The defensive-offensive.

I've wondered, since adopting the cat, if some of my gut-reactions to his behavior are due to a cyclical defensive-offensive. Could my rage be a leak, from carrying around all of that simmering symbolic thinking, that learned tendency to catastrophize?

When I screamed at my partner, when I tossed my cat off of the couch, I did not wish to hurt these beings that I love. I did not feel powerful enough to hurt them. I actually felt, I later recognized, like I was powerless. In danger. Unlistenable.

Don't we all feel a bit skittish of our own wilderness? That our unknowns are what separate us from the rest of the world, instead of what brings us into *the family of things?*

Religious Trauma Syndrome, then, has given me a name for this skittishness. Somewhere between playing Tails and now, I fell out with my idea of safety. I had to question my ultimate concerns and peel them away from their containers. The god of my upbringing had to leave his throne, and I tried to climb up there instead. The seat was far too fancy and enormous. I fell right into a crack in the velvet. I drowned in velvet and dreamt of a god that could save me from trying to be my own. I woke up and found my cat perched on my lap, as if it were a throne.

I'm learning to trust again, which is to say I'm learning to love without putting anybody or any concept back up on that throne. There's more room for all of us now. Even *the big love* doesn't have a fancy seat. Instead, I try to find its iterations in blue notes, flickers, and cracks.

One of these cracks is that Religious Trauma Syndrome is not officially a syndrome, yet. Instead of obsessing over a concrete diagnosis and fitting within its borderlines, I've learned to find comfort in ambiguity. For this particular trauma, not defining something concretely can almost be a remedy. I'd rather sit with the uncertainties than raise my voice to speak over them, insistent on a name.

A colleague of Pauline Oliveros, Roscoe Mitchell, once said in an improvisatory workshop I attended: *"Improvisation is composition, in real-time."* Improvising is not the opposite of composition, but rather the present-tense performance of it. Are we not, then, improvising in each moment, with each breath? Are we not always tethered to our ultimate concerns, singing them unconsciously?

> *I am an origin with echoes.*
> *I am an origin with echoes.*
> *I am an origin with echoes.*

Oliveros, again: *"If you're really listening, then some of the barriers can dissolve or change."*

Within my listening, I learn to play. Some of the barriers dissolve, some change. I discover the unknowns within myself—that stranger-self—unfolding with an urgency that surprises. I resist the urge to categorize them immediately within a binary of dark or light, good or bad. I acknowledge my place in the family of things, the focal-global cacophony of beings in the world. Listening in this way doesn't always sound harmonious or beautiful. But it is always a kind of survival, a kind of devotion.

And that, too, is holy.

##

EAR PIECES

after Pauline Oliveros

I.

"The first concern of all music in one way or another is to shatter the indifference of hearing, the callousness of sensibility, to create that moment of solution we call poetry, our rigidity dissolved when we occur reborn—in a sense hearing for the first time."
—Lucia Dlugoszewski

I am listening now.

I am attentive to the fault-
lines between my hearing
and my listening.

Birds—some communal, plural
some singular, or is it their proximity?
The AC unit fluttering on,
droning its way into the register of construction
down the street, which I remember from yesterday
and will hear again when I listen next.

I listen because I am an antenna in a land of appropriated radio, because I am an animal surviving, because I am a hearing person, because I wish *to dissolve the rigidity of my hearing,* because I wish to be more of what I am.

No, I do not always hear myself—
my lover next to me in bed asks if I'm okay.
He's noticed that my breathing is heavy. I wake. I labor.
I am learning to listen to what stories my breath may tell me.

I thank my ears, those flesh-antennae, those catch-and-releasers.

Since writing, I've been inside the sound of my own typing and the occasional car driving by. *Where could they all be going?*

The sound most meaningful is not singular, but the focal-global cacophony of crisp, autumn air peppered with birdsong and a crackling fire, friends drumming up strings, wood, and breath into some kind of listening-made-utterance—

As leaves reveal the sound of a silent breeze,
so people can together reveal the sound of listening.

II.

I am listening to the sounds my discomfort makes when I lay it down.

I am listening to the way my mind plays "Lay My Burden Down,"
then asks: *Which version would you like to hear?*

Hush, now—listen beyond the brain jukebox, all those associative aubades.

The trees, animated by wind, groan like ocean waves.

Listen to a memory: the way the beach sounded at sunrise when you
woke up with your mother on vacation, met the new day sunburnt,
still sticky from the one before.

Before this, a car horn beeping.
Attention snapping back to the grid.

Now, the car horn—then, the camper van's idling engine at the beach.
You hold them both. Or do they hold you?

I listen because I am awake.
If hearing is part of existence, then listening is part of my waking—
part of my willing.

I hear myself erase too hastily.
I listen to my expectations of the pencil.

I wait for my mother to call.

My ears pop at random and I don't know why.
When I listen, I stop fixating on the popping.

If there were a sound for understanding—unshrouded by language—
I'd listen to it through all sizes and shapes of shells.
I'd pass it around.

Would my mother hear it, too, through the phone speakers?
When we watched that sunrise, was she also itching?

Was she also free?

III.

Listening, again.
  I hear the things not being said.
I know the register of sigh that admits: *bullshit.*

Before this, it was a ratio of sirens-to-birdsong.
  Before that, the sound of computer keys receiving fingers.
Coasters receiving coffee cups.

Next, it'll be: *When things get back to normal, I'll—*
  All those things we were gonna do, heavier now.
Mundanity distills longing.

Because we must pay closer attention,
  I'll catch each sigh. I'll ask you how it feels.
I'll lean into the way I pull away when you answer.

If I could hear any sound I want, it would be the way
  two people that truly know one another sit, without speaking.
Not a sterile silence—a breathing quietude.

SHAPE NOTES

Cul-de-sac

late May
evenings I want
to lie down in
the middle of the
cul-de-sac a couple
streets over and feel
the warmth leave
the asphalt
underneath me
eye leveling petals
and pollen like dust
bunnies scattered
about in their
strange clusters
all the slowly
growing street lights
the only guide
back as I hear
the crickets wake
supper plates being
scraped
with a cool
breeze smell
all the laundry
of all the people
that share my zip code
but will likely
never touch

Ecclesiastes

It was my ghost, my old exhausted ghost,
that I dressed in white, and sent across the river,
weeping and weeping and weeping
inside his torn sheet.
— "Blues Skies, White Breasts, Green Trees" by Gerald Stern

Inside his torn sheet
the holy ghost becomes word,
becomes flesh,
dwells among us—

like a mailbox dwells among letters.
Like a word dwells among letters—
makes what one can of the dust
to dust, ash—to ash the blue note ashen
just by turning on the player piano.

Nobody playing what I meant to hear,
Nobody saying what I meant at all!

What I took to be a sign turned out to have no vacancy—
just my own magical thinking, shadow
puppetry on the lobe-wall again.

Blessed are the symbolic thinkers, for theirs
are the player pianos. Blessed are the magical
thinkers, for theirs is the kingdom of Disneyland.

If everything is meaningless,

then I'm a speckled something!
Out here making meaning since '92.

If everything is meaningless,
sheet-ghost at the player
piano won't cut it anymore—play
your own damn blue note, blessed one.

I Was The Exalted Exhale

The year I came out
  of organized religion,
we visited some Quaker

meetings. All silent
  and sure, you'd quake
me after, like a friend might.

Held in your gossamer-grace,
  I was unmade—tears of relief
exporting the dead

eyelash lodged there since
  last Tuesday. I was the exalted
exhale: a thread

after being pulled through
  the eye of your needle, resplendent
and of use.

Disembodied Sonnet

Sitting at your table again, I digest myself transparent—
projecting possible planets onto my plate.

The credits are already rolling; words about steps counted
and blood types materializing as my actual arms, thighs.

Those roll too, yonder and off.
My own B+ beats thicker and remembers—

just a casual colonization, nothing to cry about.
Everyone inspects everyone else's assets.

Can you gaze something into an absence?
I'm passed the sugar.

Can you sweeten something further into its own bitterness?
Into an otherworldly musk?

Just sprinkle layers and layers,
furthering it away?

Disembodied Sestina

I am new here, learning my name.
It comes in cycles, measured in waves,
then crashes against your shore as noise
expectant to be carried across borders
and arrive translated—heaping on a plate
somewhere past the salt of your understanding.

Please pass the salt, if you'll understand.
And tell me again, what is your name?
How can you spell it in grains on your plate?
The same way you pulled the main course from its waves,
breaking the rule about fishing across state borders,
Refusing to pull over when you heard the siren's noise?

Unsure of how to ratio your signal to my noise,
I adjust each stubborn antennae of my understanding.
I've heard this can be done, this transcendence of borders,
if you operate under a code name.
If you crest at the breaking point of a casual wave,
like the yolk spreading wide and thin on the plate.

Do you feel the shifting of my tectonic plates?
Is it familiar to you, that grating noise?
Evaporating from the sea, that particular tidal wave?
I'm under the bridge, I'm under/standing,
I'm dreaming of reversion to my father's name.
That's how it always went within borders.

That's how you always color in the borders.
You break apart the mosaic to earn yourself a plate.

You're polite at dinner and remember everybody's names.
You hear harmony in clinking cutlery noise
though no one communicates understanding—
and you notate it on staff paper, in longitudinal waves.

I asked, *what do you hear in my sound waves?*
You said, *it's a music without borders.*
I think we've reached an understanding.
We've at last excavated our inherited plates.
Our tributaries each feed the feast, feed the noise.
The feedback isn't signaling our names.

Understanding rambles on, and occasionally waves.
Not so concerned with what name you assign to her borders.
She tunes into the sound of a plate receiving salt—that tiny, holy noise.

Will the Circle Be Unbroken?

Peggy paints Nashville's buildings before they get torn down. The one of J&J's Market and Cafe has bits of glass she found in the street and stuck in the canvas, as well as a tiny bit of a mirror: *You can find your eye in the reflection there, you'll know it's your eye when you blink,* she says. I find my nose ring first, shining on Broadway where the pedal taverns probably are now. I show her my tattoo of the J&Js sign on my thigh. She says, *That's an acute angle on an acute thigh!* We eat our fish with melted butter and discover that we both love hymns. Later, when we sing "Will the Circle Be Unbroken?" she thinks of her mother, who passed on a *cold and cloudy day* just like it says in the first verse. When I sing that song, I think of Willie Nelson, *Benny and Joon*, and Venn diagrams. *I'm always thinking of Venn diagrams,* I tell Peggy. She reaches over the table and picks up a beautiful box with three intersecting circles painted on it and she says, *Like this?* She didn't know they had a name. I tell her they were named after John Venn, who was a priest before he decided to be a logician instead. I ask her if she's heard the verse in "Will The Circle Be Unbroken?" that talks about singing secular songs after being raised to sing hymns. I try to paraphrase it, but I'll include it here now: *You remember songs of heaven / Which you sang with childish voice / Do you love the hymns they taught you / Or are songs of earth your choice?* We drink sangria and sing "Dark Reverie," which Peggy is quick to point out is not a reverie at all. She won't let me leave without giving me dessert, and spoons cherry yogurt atop cheesecake like a total genius. I eat happily.

Hatching

Watching you sleep,
your face becomes
landscape:
I've imagined tiny snow-skiers
dotting the slopes of your
brow, nose, lips—
sojourning your vastness.
Your walking-around
and the thoughts in your head
have begun to dance:
Perpetually in balance,
I've seen it—
Those tiny snow-skiers like
carrier pigeons
between your head
and heart and feet
at the grocery store
and in your bed.
Where my walking-around
meets my innermost
is where my ecstasy belongs:
and that is where you've been—
It's a weekday sort of thing,
our walking and our questioning,
our answering and
our breakfast.

Slow Morning Crow

The third alarm goes off— the one that's not messing around. No more fake marimbas. You roll over, your legs hatching from the comforter like clockwork. That's how I know it's actually time to wake up — your legs sticking out like that, dappled generously with morning light. It's got work to do yet. Your gaze finds me, moans me open like a morning-glory. I'd like to tell you something you don't already know, but you've known that from the beginning. We might wake with more malaise baked into our cheap sheets every day for the rest of it. But I'll be here, measuring the crust of sleep around your eyes. I'll notice the drool unspooled from dream-thread on your pillowcase and celebrate it. That means you really got to escape, and I was the one cheering you on from my own pillow, mouth-breathing again. This is the way the world begins, here in our nest, with a slow morning crow. You are no farmer nor shepherd but you could have been, for you rise when you must, tend to your keep.

Alarmist Apology

I'm sorry I did not exhale for a moment there.
   It was incredible: like a hot pan without

oil, I was sizzling without a subject and burning
   us both, setting off the fire alarm again.

Now I can see that you will cook with me again
   anyway, and that is indelible: I will always remember

the way you used the kitchen towel to hush the alarm
   back into slumber again.

Ad Tendere: **An Elegy for David Berman**

Moments can be monuments to you / if your life is interesting and true
— "People" by Silver Jews

>Who am I to grieve, only
>>knowing you in moment-
>
>monuments: bits of lint
>>clinging to ear-buds on lunch break
>
>walks, picked off and ceremoniously
>>inserted? Or, the time I watched you
>
>obtusely scoot your chair up to the foot
>>of the stage, middle of the crowd,
>
>unaware (or uncaring) of people staring
>>as your flip-phone emerged, capturing
>
>Cassie singing. Then, a broken cable
>>during the second song, she came to the front
>
>of the stage and sat: singing and playing
>>unamplified, out of the light's reach.
>
>Everyone looked like you had when we scooted
>>forward, too, leaning toward her voice
>
>evaporating into warehouse ether.
>>Enveloped by a space that hadn't existed

before—for anyone but you, you who didn't

        wait for the power to go out to light a candle

to be more there.

Transaction in Technicolor

How can I help you,
soaked in palpable thunder?

An inevitable weather: vacuuming
color out of the lenses at the borders

of our understanding, imprisoning
the prism of unknowns.

Meanwhile, I perch on
advantageous clouds, reading

the times ticking away, asking
them: *What size?* Asking

form of payment, going home
to make dinner, to make rapture.

When those chaotic patterns reflect
through my home and onto the wall,

I take notes. Like, *we all work together
with a giggle-and-a-grin!*

Or we all write together with a poem about
the grocery store, because it could be some

great = sign, but that is a little secondary
to death, now don't you think?

No, probably nothing is a sign, my dear
stormchaser! Write what you—no, your cloud

communes in this symphonic weathering,
revealing its vapor, an inflammation of empathy.

A protest song in the heat of more like
hymnology: when saying *I love you*

became like saying *ROYGBIV*.
Was it identification of a spectrum of light,

or acknowledgement of a naturally-occuring
principle?

Let There Be

*"The actual theological meaning of the word "salvation" is meaning.
To seek salvation is to seek a sense of meaning to the world, one's life."*
—Fanny Howe

In the beginning, there was evangelizing on the playground.
Age five and confident The Spirit   would move:
Have you asked Jesus into your heart? my
How do you do? and almost as casual.

Winded by the   merry   go   round, Christ
on my tongue and
cherry-sweet.
*
Next, the pastor handing over his Mastercard
and emphatic: *Jesus put all,*
all our debt
on his   credit card.

He'd later fire my father from working at the church.
Next, my father's heavy sighs.
*
Frank Zappa said the Shaggs were better than the Beatles,
but their manager-father
chased after Helen's husband with a gun
after he discovered that she'd married.
The police told her to pick one of the men to belong to.

She was the drummer, and never in time.
*
In the beginning of last year's Halloween party,

The Shaggs cover band was taken more seriously
in costume than the Wiggin sisters
playing at their best.
*

Start over, with the Shaggs' "It's Halloween":
> *It's time for games*
> *It's time for fun*
> *Not for just one*
> *But for everyone*

*

    It's Halloween
and I'm fall, costumed in leaves.
Or rather, camouflaged? Falling still.

Last night's panic attack still trickling through
the gutters of my breath—minutes 'til closing time.

> The woman from Japan races back into the lobby,
> motioning for the phone.

> After calling someone to jump her car,
> she tells me my leaf-crown makes me look like a queen.

The next day she brings me chocolates
and says: *You are my goddess of safe.*
*

In the beginning, Leonard Cohen singing:
There is a crack in everything
That's how the light gets in.

I begin with Cohen's last:
You Want It Darker,

*
St. Hildegard of Bingen claimed to receive visions of God's love,
manifesting in *living sparks*.

When she died, her sisters saw two pillars of light shoot
through the sky and into the room.
*
If there's any possible way, I begin with
Let there be light.

##

SOURCES

1. Image on p. 3, accompanying "Hymnology Class"[1]

2. "Ear Piece" (1998) by Pauline Oliveros[2]:

    1. Are you listening now?
    2. Are you listening to what you are now hearing?
    3. Are you hearing while you listen?
    4. Are you listening while you are hearing?
    5. Do you remember the last sound you heard before this question?
    6. What will you hear in the near future?
    7. Can you hear now and also listen to your memory of an old sound?
    8. What causes you to listen?
    9. Do you hear yourself in your daily life?
    10. Do you have healthy ears?
    11. If you could hear any sound you want, what would it be?
    12. Are you listening to sounds now or just hearing them?
    13. What sound is most meaningful to you?

---

[1] Detail from Original sacred harp (Denson revision) / Benjamin Franklin White [hymnal]. Haleyville: Sacred Harp Pub. Co., 1936.

[2] Oliveros, Pauline. *Deep Listening: A Composer's Sound Practice*. IUniverse, 2005.

3. The first volume of "American Harmony" by Nym Cooke[3] and the Sacred Harp Musical

4. "Skittish of Our Own Wilderness" includes quotes from Mary Oliver's *Upstream,*[4] Pauline Oliveros' *Deep Listening: A Composer's Sound Practice*, and Paul Tillich's *Dynamics of Faith*[5].

5. "Transaction in Technicolor" includes a quote from Woody Guthrie's "All Work Together."

6. "Let There Be" includes a quote from Leonard Cohen's "Anthem."

---

[3] Cooke, Nym. *American Harmony: Inspired Choral Miniatures from New England, Appalachia, the Mid-Atlantic, the South, and the Midwest*. Vol. 1, David R. Godine, 2017.
[4] Oliver, Mary. *Upstream: Selected Essays.* Penguin Books, 2019.
[5] Tillich, Paul. *Dynamics of Faith*. HarperOne, 2009.

ACKNOWLEDGEMENTS

Thank you to C. M. Tollefson at Cathexis Northwest Press, where "Hatching" first appeared.

"Alarmist Apology" and "Will the Circle Be Unbroken?" appear in song-form on my album, *Songs for John Venn* (via SPINSTER).

Thank you to the following for being a listening presence to this book: Katie Miller, Jackie Zeisloft, Hilary Bell, Susannah Felts, AM Ringwalt, and most of all, Trevor Nikrant.